B53 053 650 4

KT-513-392

This Book Belongs To

· ·

To all of the wonderful team at Belle & Boo,
thank you for helping me create an enchanting
world for everyone to enjoy, and for all the
fun we have had along the way

ORCHARD BOOKS
338 Euston Road, London NW1 3BH
Orchard Books Australia
Level 17/207 Kent Street, Sydney, NSW 2000

First published in 2013 by Orchard Books

First published in paperback in 2013

ISBN 978 1 40832 089 1

Text by Gillian Shields
Text © Orchard Books 2013
Illustrations © Mandy Sutcliffe 2013

The right of Mandy Sutcliffe to be identified as the illustrator of this work
has been asserted by her in accordance with the Copyright, Designs and Patents Act, 1988.

With thanks to Mark Burgess

A CIP catalogue record for this book is available from the British Library.

1 3 5 7 9 10 8 6 4 2

Printed in China

Orchard Books is a division of Hachette Children's Books,
an Hachette UK company.
www.hachette.co.uk

ROTHERHAM LIBRARY SERVICE	
B53053650	
Bertrams	04/06/2013
JF	£6.99
KIM	

Belle & Boo

and the

Yummy Scrummy Day

Mandy Sutcliffe

ORCHARD

This is **Belle**, and this is **Boo**.

They are always together –
on sunny days,
rainy days,
and dreamy let's-be-lazy days.

"This is a hungry sort of day," sighed Boo, patting his tummy.
"What would you like for breakfast?" smiled Belle.

"Cookies and cake," said Boo.

"Boo!" Belle laughed. "You can't just eat cake."

"Not even carrot cake?" asked Boo, hopefully.

"There are lots of other yummy things to eat," Belle said.

"What sort of things?" asked Boo.

"Well," said Belle, "what about porridge?"

"Ouch!" said Boo. "Too hot!"

"Toast?"

"Too crunchy," said Boo, shaking his head.

"A speckled boiled egg?"

"Too . . . *eggy*," said Boo.

"Oh, Boo!" said Belle.

Then, she had a splendid idea that might just work . . .

"Let's make this a **yummy, scrummy day**," she said.
"I'll make a feast for Snuffly Elephant, Yellow Duck
and Honey Bear, and you can help me."

"A feast!" Boo exclaimed. "Will there be cake?"
"Not today," laughed Belle.
"Oh," said Boo, looking disappointed.

Belle got her basket and they went into the garden.

In the far corner, behind the cherry tree, was the vegetable patch.

"We'll need some carrots, Boo," said Belle.

"Hooray!" said Boo, and he sang a happy song.

"Carrots are yummy, carrots are fun,
I like to have carrot cake in my tum!
Carrots are orange, carrots are long,
And this is my carroty-rabbitty song!"

"No carrot cake today," said Belle, as she filled her basket with vegetables.

Boo began to feel worried. He was getting very hungry.

Boo followed Belle to the orchard.

She picked some apples and plums.

"Oooh, can I pick some blackberries?" asked Boo.

"Be careful of the prickles!" said Belle.

Boo was good at dodging the prickles and finding the fattest blackberries.

And he liked having purple paws!

"Picking fruit is fun," Boo said. "But I won't eat any."

"You don't have to," said Belle, kindly.

"Good," said Boo. "Too fruity."

Back in the kitchen, they put all the vegetables in a
lovely big pot of soup. Belle stuffed the apples with
plums and blackberries and sparkling brown sugar.

Boo was getting **hungrier** and **hungrier**.

His tummy started to rumble. And then something
surprising happened. The bubbling soup and baked
apples started to smell . . .

. . . interesting.

Boo sniffed.

Belle smiled.

Perhaps her plan was starting to work . . .

At last, Belle served the feast in her best tea set.
Snuffly Elephant, Yellow Duck and Honey Bear
looked very happy.

Boo was secretly longing to taste everything.

But Belle said, "You don't have to eat, Boo. You don't like soup."

"I know," said Boo, unhappily. "Too soupy."

But it smelt so good! And the baked apples
looked so juicy and sweet!

Then, Boo had a perfectly brilliant idea.
He scampered away . . .

. . . and found some very useful **dressing-up** things.

A few minutes later, a stranger arrived.

He had tall wobbly legs, a thick golden mane
and a long swishy tail.

"I am Mr Lion," said the stranger, in a funny deep voice.
"I'm a new toy."

"Come and join the feast!" said Belle with a smile.

"Ooh, yummy!" said the lion. "I mean, I'd be delighted."

Mr Lion ate two big bowls of soup
and three sticky baked apples.

"That was splendid," he sighed. "Thank you!
But . . . um . . . I have to go now."

He began to hurry away.

"Please don't go yet, Mr Lion," said Belle.

"Please stay and tell us a story about lions.

Or sing a lion song.

Or," she laughed, "do a lion dance."

"A lion dance?" said Mr Lion.

"Oh, dear . . . oh, help . . . oh, very well."

He began to do a strange, wobbly dance,
waggling his golden mane from side to side.

But then he started to spin faster and faster
on his tall wobbly legs . . .

until he wibbled . . .

and wobbled . . .

and . . .

CRASH!

"Oh, Boo!" said Belle. "Are you all right?"

"Very extra-specially all right," Boo replied, happily.
"Very yummy scrummy all right. I do like veggie-bobbly soup
and fruity things after all."

"I'm so glad, Boo!" said Belle, with a big smile.
"Would you like a cookie now?"

"No, thank you," said Boo . . .

"I'm too full!"

Carefully tear along the line to remove your Belle & Boo print. Remember to ask an adult to help you make these biscuits.

Special Spiced Biscuits

170g golden syrup
70g brown sugar
60g butter
290g plain flour
2 teaspoons mixed spice

Preheat your oven to 180c.

Put the **golden syrup, brown sugar** and **butter** in a pan.

Stir
over a low heat until melted and smooth.

Leave to cool to room temperature.

Put the **flour** and mixed **spice** in a large mixing bowl. Add the cooled **syrup** mixture and stir well to combine.

Roll the dough
to a flat 2mm thickness.

Use a biscuit cutter to cut out shapes and place on a greased baking tray.

Bake in
the oven for 7 minutes . . .

. . . or until the biscuits have turned golden.